Fun Under Your Border Terrier Puppy and Dog

By Vince Stead

Copyright

© 2013 by Vince Stead

All rights reserved. No part of this book may be reproduced or transmitted in any form or by any means, electronic or mechanical, including photocopying, recording, or by any information storage and retrieval system, without permission in writing from the copyright owner.

Contents

Copyright 2
1. The Characteristics of a Border Terrier Dog 7
2. What You Should Know About Puppy Teeth ... 11
3. How to Select Treats to Train Your Dog With .. 13
4. Some Helpful Tips for Raising Your Border Terrier Puppy 15
5. Are Rawhide Treats Good for Your Border Terrier? 21
6. How to Crate Train Your Border Terrier 23
7. When Should You Spay or Neuter Your Dog? . 25
8. When Your Border Terrier Makes Potty Mistakes 27
9. How to Teach Your Border Terrier to Fetch ... 31
10. Make it Easier and Healthier for Feeding Your Border Terrier 35
11. When Your Border Terrier Has Separation Anxiety, and How to Deal With It 37
12. When Your Border Terrier is Afraid of Loud Noises 41
13. How to Stop Your Border Terrier from Jumping Up on People 45
14. How to Build a Whelping Box for an Border Terrier or Any Other Breed of Dog 47
15. How to Teach Your Border Terrier to Sit 49
16. Why Your Border Terrier Needs a Good Soft Bed to Sleep In 51

17. How to Stop Your Border Terrier from Running Away or Bolting Out the Door _____ 53

18. Some Helpful Tips for Raising Your Border Terrier Puppy_____ 57

19. How to Socialize Your Border Terrier Puppy _____ 63

20. How to Stop Your Border Terrier Dog from Excessive Barking _____ 71

21. When Your Border Terrier Has Dog Food or Toy Aggression Tendencies_____ 77

22. What You Should Know About Fleas and Ticks _____ 81

23. How to Stop Your Border Terrier Puppy or Dog from Biting _____ 85

24. What to Expect Before and During Your Dog Having Puppies_____ 87

25. What the Benefits of Micro Chipping Your Dog Are to You_____ 93

26. How to Get Something Out of a Puppy or Dog's Belly without Surgery _____ 97

27. How to Clean Your Border Terrier s Ears Correctly_____ 99

28. How to Stop Your Border Terrier from Eating Their Own Stools _____ 101

29. How Invisible Fencing Typically Works to Train and Protect Your Dog_____ 103

30. Some Items You Should Never Let Your Puppy or Dog Eat_____ 107

31. How to Make Sure Your Dog is Eating a Healthy Amount of Food _____ 109

32. Make it Easier and Healthier for Feeding Your Border Terrier _____ 111

33. How to Clean and Groom Your Border Terrier _____ 113

34. How to Trim a Puppy or Dogs Nails Properly _____ 117

35. The 5 Different Kinds of Worms That Can Harm Your Dog _____ 121

36. How to Deworm Your Border Terrier for Good Health _____ 125

37. What You Should Know About Dog Rabies 127

38. Some Helpful Healthy and Tasty Homemade Dog Food Recipes _____ 131

1. The Characteristics of a Border Terrier Dog

The Border Terrier is a very nice dog that loves to be a part of the family circle. They are not as spunky as other terrier breeds, but they do still have their own minds about them, which sometimes makes them stubborn and not very obedient when you want them to be. They are active, athletic dogs who need daily exercise to stay healthy and in shape. They have a high energy drive and are happy when they have something to do to keep them from becoming bored.

The Border Terrier was originally used for hunting foxes, rodents, otters, and badgers. In the olden days farmers had trouble with foxes killing their livestock, so the Border Terrier helped with the problem. They were developed in the 18th century. The Border Terrier was not recognized by Britain's Kennel Club until the early 20th century. In 1920 the Border Terrier Club of America was formed and in 1930 they were recognized by the American Kennel Club. Today Border Terriers are mostly used as companion dogs and family dogs.

The Border Terrier is a small, medium-bonded breed. Their body is narrow, and so are their shoulders. Their muzzle is short, their eyes are black, and their teeth meet in a scissor like bite. Their ears are triangle shaped dropping forward.

Their eyes are a dark hazel color. They have a double coat that comes in red, tan, grizzle and blue and tan, or wheaten, and sometimes with white on their chest. The average height for a male Border Terrier is about 13 to 16 inches and the average height for a female is 11 to 14 inches usually. The average weight for a male Border Terrier is about 13 to 16 pounds and the average weight for a female is 11 to 14 pounds respectively.

The Border Terriers coat needs to brushed weekly and professionally groomed two times a year at least. They shed little to no hair hardly, and their coat is good for those with allergies, and some people like to call it hypoallergenic. You should clean their ears and brush their teeth to prevent any infections. Bathe them only when it is necessary to do so.

The average life expectancy for a Border Terrier is about 15 or more years on average. They are a generally a very healthy breed, but can run into some health problems like all other dogs can get sometimes, like: Hip dysplasia, Perthes disease, seizures, juvenile cataracts, various heart defects, Progressive retinal atrophy, and more.

They are very even tempered, and are friendly and are rarely aggressive, even though they are stubborn sometimes. They are very good with children, so that makes them very good house pets, but they may chase around other family pets, so make sure you socialize them first. They take to training for tasks very well, but seem less trainable when taught only just tricks. Because of their intelligence, and good tempered nature, and willingness to work, the Border Terrier can adapt to life in any environment almost, and are very content with being with a family most of all.

2. What You Should Know About Puppy Teeth

There is no doubt about it; puppies are going to chew on things! Dogs will have 28 baby teeth, and 42 permanent teeth. When a puppy is roughly 2 to 3 weeks old, their baby teeth start to come in. All their baby teeth should be in place by roughly 8 weeks of age.

The puppy's new teeth are very tiny and sharp, and will hurt your fingers when they get a hold of them. Most mothers will start to wean their babies at 5 to 6 weeks old.

Your puppies baby teeth will start to come out around 8 to 12 weeks of age. By roughly 8 months old, your dog's permanent teeth should all be in. You should make sure that all baby teeth are out, so that a tooth does not get left in, and another one comes in and crowds the space, and also gives your dog pain. You would need to visit the vet if you see this happening.

Your puppy is going to want to chew on something, just like a real baby, their teeth are coming in, and they want to relieve some of the pain. It is good for them to chew, to help the teeth come thru. You would want to get some appropriate chew items to help them.

You could start to train your dog to have their teeth brushed. You can pick up doggie tooth supplies at your local pet store usually, and get down and dirty and brush your doggy's teeth. Rawhide chews are an excellent source of good tooth hygiene, as they are good for your dog's teeth, and can help take off build up plaque, and dogs usually love it also!

A lot of puppies and dogs end up getting human food usually from the weakest link in the family. If your dog is under the table, they usually will go to the person they think will mostly likely give them some food scraps. If you do, just remember, chocolate and some nuts can kill your dog, never give chocolate. Raisins can be just as deadly for your dog, do not give, they can shut down your dog's kidneys, so be very careful of these products and your puppy or dog.

3. How to Select Treats to Train Your Dog With

Dogs need to be rewarded the way we humans love being treated. Would you like someone hanging a treat over you, and then just patting you on the head for a good round of tricks shown? The answer is obviously a NO! The same thing happens if you do that to your pet, he gets de motivated and annoyed as well. He would not trust you the next time around if he doesn't have an incentive to bank on.

You may have seen your friend or neighbor offering treats to their dogs for a good job done. But remember, your dog needs one, but maybe not the same treat as other dogs. Some dogs would love a certain treat, while others wouldn't care for that treat as much as a different kind. They would certainly want more than what the other dog is getting at the moment. Now this is left up to the owner to figure out, you have to understand your dog's likes and dislikes. Change the levels of the treat rewards for your dog, so that he understands why he gets what he gets.

Level One: Here you should give him a reward for the job he is willing to do, not for standing on his head or back flips. This reward should be a standard treat for all the goodness he does for you. You can consider this to be like his daily wage.

Level Two: Your dog would want this reward more than the first one, since it is for something special or a special occasion for which he would get this. This reward should be kept when he does something extra special while undergoing obedience training. Treat this reward as overtime for the little angel, he would appreciate it, and would be more motivated to work harder and smarter next time.

Level Three: This is for emergencies such as situations that would involve life and death for example. You should train your dog on how to rescue folks around in grave situations, or maybe even be man's best friend in times of emotional need. Here the treats would signify higher amounts of love and dedication towards him. He would understand that this treat is meant for something serious and not just because he chased the next door neighbor's cat off your property.

It's not about the size of the treat: Now the size of the treat doesn't matter here, it's the intent which does. While handing out treats to your dog, you should pat him on the head, which will tell him he is worth the treat being given. It's now up to you on what treats you best think your little doggie should get.

4. Some Helpful Tips for Raising Your Border Terrier Puppy

Before you bring your Border Terrier puppy home, you might want to get things ready for him or her. Some of the things you might want to get would include:

Some dog crates: one or two for the house, and one for the car. You would want to get some fencing for the back yard, and as you know, Border Terrier are going to be really big dogs when they grow up! You might as well get the heaviest duty dog gear you can buy, it will be worth it!

You would want to get your home and yard ready just like you would for a new baby almost. You would want to puppy proof your home, nothing that would hurt the puppy should be out, and all cabinets should be locked.

For outside the house, all pools and hot tubs should be fenced in, and all gates should be locked and double checked. A Border Terrier can really put a lot of weight into something, if you think they might get out, they probably can, so make it even tougher, it's a Border Terrier !

Collars and leashes: you would actually need several for training purposes. A short one for training and a long one for walks you go on. You should not leave a collar on a puppy while unsupervised, it could get caught and choke the puppy.

A collar should be used only when training, but they are common on most every dog, just make sure you have a good fitting one, and watch your puppy, to make sure he or she does not get it caught. A collar should not be left on, but dog owners do it all the time it seems, so just be extra careful.

You should never have to yell or scream, or get carried away when trying to train your Border Terrier. If you feel he or she is not moving forward, take a break, and try it again in a bit. Make sure you are not the one who is trying too hard. To puppy will learn the commands over time. No puppy gets it all right the first time, there will be mistakes, but in the long run, you will have a much better trained dog. One you and your family can live with for many years to come!

While your puppy is still young, you should enroll yourself and your new puppy in as many dog obedient classes that you think you could handle. This will be the best experience for both you and your puppy, and you both will bond much better together, and get the most out of it. For the long haul, it is totally worth it!

Hopefully your puppy has already seen the vet before you even brought him home, just for a checkup at least. You should at this time, find a reputable vet in your area, and set your new puppy up for regular visits and exams all puppies and dogs need to have on a regular basis.

The first day you bring you new puppy home, try to make it when you have plenty of time off of work or school, so that the puppy is not immediately left alone and insecure. It is best to spend plenty of time with the new puppy, especially the first couple of days.

If you can take a sock or towel with you, and let the mother and any other siblings roll around on it, it would be a good comfort blanket to help your new puppy adjust in his new home.

Your puppy might whine, whimper and cry the first couple of nights, this is natural really. It will go away eventually, as this is how the baby is raised by its mother. It whines when it cries for its mother when it wants to eat, and is crying out for attention.

That is where the towel or sock with the mothers scent rubbed on it comes in handy to put inside the crate. You would also want some good solid stainless steel bowls for food and water. You should check with your vet on a proper food and feeding time, usually twice daily, at the same times, but some vets recommend different diets for your Border Terrier , so check with your vet first.

Teach your new Border Terrier puppy to be a part of the family. Border Terrier dogs like to be included with the family; they are not that happy if just left in the back yard. They like to be included with the family, so keep that in mind and have fun with your new Border Terrier puppy!

You can teach your new puppy to go to the bathroom outside. You need to take your new puppy outside several times a day. A puppy cannot tell you when they have to go pee or poop, they just go. It is your responsibility to know to take the puppy outside, since they will have to go to the bathroom several times each day.

When you take your new puppy outside, teach them to eliminate in a certain spot, and then give them a treat and praise. Continue to do this each time you take them outside, tell them to go "potty" and wait for them to go. As soon as they are done, reward them with praise and a treat, and take them back inside.

When you take your puppy outside to go to the bathroom, when you take him or her out, just stand still, and let the dog do their business. When they are finally doing their business, while they are doing it, just stand there and say, "Good Potty" "Good Baby" and talk sweet to them, until they are done.

When they are done, give them praise and a treat. Continue doing this until you only use praise, and the dog will learn to go outside and do his or her businesses quickly, and then back inside.

Under no circumstances should you ever leave your new puppy unsupervised. If you have to do something, he or she should be in their crate safe and sound.

5. Are Rawhide Treats Good for Your Border Terrier?

By all means, give your dog some rawhide treats! They are good for them, and dogs love them! Rawhide is great for cleaning your dog's teeth, and it also gives your Border Terrier something to chew on, besides your couch or favorite pair of shoes!

When looking at rawhide, try to find the biggest pieces, because you don't want the smaller bone fragments that break off the smaller ones for your Border Terrier . You would be smart to ask your vet, or shop around for the best quality rawhide you can find. It comes in many different styles, and even fun filled treats inside some of them, to keep your Border Terrier entertained!

It is best to supervise your dog with a rawhide chew, as it could come apart and get lodged in the dog's throat, but that is extremely rare, but still could happen. Just as any toy or treat you give your pet, should be supervised.

When your dog has chewed on a big piece of rawhide, and it is soft and gooey, take it away, and give them a new one. Let the old one harden up again, and you can give it back to them later.

The good thing about rawhide is it is good for your Border Terrier's stress level. A bored Border Terrier will have more stress, because he or she is bored, and a rawhide treat will keep them more occupied and entertained!

It is hard to tell if good rawhide comes from the United States, or other countries, so it is best to get the best quality you can find.

6. How to Crate Train Your Border Terrier

If you were a new Border Terrier puppy, wouldn't you want your new home to be warm, comfortable, secure and inviting! Sure you would, and your new Border Terrier puppy, or even a full grown older dog, loves a nice secure home to sleep in!

You want your Border Terrier puppy or dog to have a secure place to rest and go to, when you want them to be in a secure place while you're away.

To begin with a new puppy, you would want to have a good size crate, one they can stand up and lie down in, and turn around comfortably, but not to big either.

You would want to leave the door open in the beginning, and just get your Border Terrier used to the crate. You would put a treat at the opening of the crate, and let your puppy or dog go and eat it. You would continue until you are putting the treats in the back of the crate, and your Border Terrier feels comfortable going inside.

You want them to get used to getting a treat for going inside, and then later turn it into praise. This will be their home. You would put their food and water inside, and with training, it will become their own little den, a place they like to sleep.

After you have your Border Terrier going inside, it is time to shut the door jut for a very short period of time, 1 to 2 minutes. You would give your Border Terrier a treat while inside, and praise, then open the door back up. You never want to use the crate as punishment. Don't put them in the crate when they have been bad. They will associate that with being put in the crate, and you want them to feel good and secure in their spot.

Put their crate out of the way, but not totally out of the way. Somewhere in a room the family shares, but in his or her own little corner, make it a nice home for them.

If you are going to be gone, and have to leave your Border Terrier in his crate for a long period of time, try to get them their favorite toys. A toy with a snack inside, that takes time to get out, so they are occupied for a while, because you want them to associate going into their crate, as a fun place to go.

7. When Should You Spay or Neuter Your Dog?

If you want to know when you should spray or neuter your dog, please read on and learn more. When the ovarian hysterectomy of the female species is described, it is called spraying. On the other hand castrating a male species is known as neutering. Both are surgical treatments and can be done by a qualified veterinarian. This makes the dog incapable of having babies in future. The procedure is very beneficial for you and your dog.

When is the right time to spray or neuter?: When the dog is as early as 8 weeks old, the procedure can be done easily, by a qualified vet. It is strongly recommended that they get the neutering done early, since it would be healthier for your dog, and the dog population doesn't increase.

Is it important to have your dog neutered? Yes it is important to have your dog neutered. Take a look at the animal shelters around; there numbers are increasing and the population of dogs with them increasing by the day. Would you rather have the current dogs neutered and avoid over population or would you want them to grow only to be left out and euthanized later on? Not everyone is a willing adopter, due to many reasons. Some even abandon their pets, again for various reasons, hence neutering your pet helps.

The health and behavioral benefits: When you neuter the dog, he would live a happy life and a longer life, not to forget a healthier life. When you spray the dog, she would be devoid of the mating heat crying syndrome, when she is in heat. Plus there is a lot of mess when the dog is in heat, and she would thank you dearly for getting her sprayed on time, which avoids such a mess.

When you neuter the male, he wouldn't have sexual desires, he would not mark the furniture and the walls with his urine, there wouldn't be aggressiveness in him, nor would he want to roman wild and aimlessly.

For females, when you spray them, the chances of getting breast cancer (yes it happens to dogs as well) in the first heat cycle is minimized and prevented altogether. She also would be saved from uterine cancer and infections as well.

When you neuter the males, it would prevent cancer of the testicles and his prostate gland wouldn't enlarge, so the risk of having perianal tumors can be ruled out.

Hopefully now you might understand why neutering and spraying the dog would be good for them. Always speak to your vet and then make a decision on whether the pet needs to be neutered or not.

8. When Your Border Terrier Makes Potty Mistakes

Too many dogs have been abandoned at animal shelters, just for the sole purpose of the dog making potty mistakes in the wrong places, and not being properly trained.

Border Terrier's sometimes might go potty in response to fear, excitement, separation anxiety, marking territory, and sometimes medical problems. It is best to start with your vet about any medical problems, before you move forward. Some dogs may have a urinary infection. Spayed females may have some small leaking at times where they lie down or sleep.

One of the most common symptoms is separation anxiety. If the dog has gone thru some new changes, or there has been a change in the household, it could be affecting your Border Terrier.

Another problem might be submissive urination, which occurs when your dog first sees you when you come home. They may exhibit uncontrollable urinating and submissive behavior, like rolling on his or her back.

One way to help remedy this, is to immediately take your Border Terrier outside right when you get home, and try to stay calm and low beat when just greeting your dog, to help him or her get less excited.

Some dogs will perform a marking behavior by lifting their hind leg and urinating. This is most common in unneutered male dogs that have not been neutered. If a male dog is neutered around 6 months of age, this will usually cure this behavior. A male dog should be neutered if he is not intended for breeding, or there is a medical reason while your dog should not be neutered.

If you see your Border Terrier getting ready to go potty, immediately clap your hands together, or use another device to get their attention, and immediately take them outside.

A dog is not considered housebroken until he or she has not had an accident for around 45 days in a row. You can easily train your young Border Terrier to go outside; when you notice that he or she is sniffing around like they want to go. After they just ate, had a bath, just woke up, or just your gut instinct that your Border Terrier might go potty inside.

If you need to be gone from your Border Terrier for an extended period of time, you should keep him or her in a crate or cage. Make sure you do not give them an oversize crate or cage, or they will use that space to go potty.

If you need to train an adult Border Terrier, do it just like you would a puppy! Give them the right guidance, and train them just like you would a puppy. An adult dog needs to urinate roughly 3 to 4 times a day, and defecate once or twice daily.

When your puppy or adult Border Terrier does a bad thing inside, in a firm and stern voice, say "Bad Dog", and then take then outside where you would like them to go, and tell them "Good Dog." Give praise when your Border Terrier goes outside.

To potty train a puppy or adult dog, you must lay down newspapers, and bring the puppy to the newspapers, and say "Good Dog" at that spot. When you catch your puppy starting to go, get them if you still can, and tell them "Bad Dog", and then put them on the newspaper, and tell them "Good Dog", and after they go, give them praise.

You would start out with a wide section of newspapers on the floor in the beginning, and then slowly you can decrease the size to a manageable spot. Give your Border Terrier a little time to get used to this. They will learn to go on the newspapers when they get praise. Use a stern voice when they go in the wrong spot, they would rather have praise, and will learn to go on the newspapers!

9. How to Teach Your Border Terrier to Fetch

Dogs and owners usually love a good game of fetch. Especially if your dog brings the item back to you, and gives it to you, or drops it at your feet. Playing fetch is a great way to spend quality time with your puppy or dog.

You can easily teach your puppy or dog to fetch with a few simple commands. Dogs used to be taught to fetch, so that they could help police and others fetch guns and drugs from the bad guys.

One of the best ways to teach your puppy or dog to fetch is to use 2 identical toys. This is called the bait and switch system.

What you would do is hide one of the toys on your person, and then toss the other toy away from you, not too far in the beginning, so that your dog can visually keep an eye on the object.

You would keep your dog on his or her leash, since you want them to chase the object when you give the word fetch, not when they see you throw it. They should not leave until the command of fetch is given to them.

You would hide one of the toys on your body, then toss the other toy away, and then unleash your dog, and tell them to fetch. When your dog goes and gets the toy, and brings it back by you, but does not drop it. You pull out the other toy, and pretend like that is the fun toy to have, and then get your dog to want that toy instead. When they drop the toy in their mouth, you throw the other toy, and say fetch again, and pick up the toy they dropped when the run off again.

If your dog is not toy motivated, you could try rubbing some of their favorite food product on it, and then trying it that way, it will be hard for aw dog to resist when it is slimmed with their favorite food product.

If your dog does not take to any of the fetch play, then you might have to force them to fetch. You would do this, by throwing the toy, and saying fetch, and if your dog does not move, you physically walk them over to the toy, and wait by the toy, until the dog picks it up, and if you have meat spread on it, they will pick it up, or change their favorite food on it. When your dog picks up the toy, gives lots of praise for doing a good job.

You should find good items to play fetch with your dog with. A stick you find in the woods is not the best thing, when your dog is running with it, it can get stuck in the ground and jab them, and it can also have disease and germs from the actual tree it came from.

It is best to start out with small throws, so your dog can visually see the item, and you won't have to walk as far, if your dog does not cooperate in the beginning, and you have to teach him or her for a bit, before they pick it up. Once you have your dog fetching for you, it will be a sport you both love and cherish.

10. Make it Easier and Healthier for Feeding Your Border Terrier

You can make is much easier on your Border Terrier when it comes to eating. Some dogs you can leave their food out for them, and they do not over eat. Other dogs may over eat until they get bloated, or they gobble it down super-fast, and have gas problems and more serious problems.

To find out how much your dog should be eating, you should check with your vet. You could also measure your dog's food, and then feed him or her twice a day. If they eat the whole bowl, give them more next time, if they don't eat it all, give them less each time. You could measure it, and then come up with the right amount for your dog for each meal.

For dogs that gobble down their food so fast, the pet supply places sell dog bowls that have inserts in the bowl, so the dog would have to slow down to eat. You would never want to give your dog just one meal a day. You should feed them twice a day, and at the same time each day, so they can count on their schedule, just like people seem to love, breakfast, lunch and dinner!

For large size dogs, it is harder on them and their joints when they have to bend over to get their head down to the ground to get a drink of water, and that is bad for their joints, especially if they are young still. Some pet supply stores sell water and food bowls that go in a stand and make it higher off the ground, and that makes it easier for your puppy or dog to swallow, as their body is more parallel to the ground while eating.

A raised water and eating bowl, will make your dog more comfortable when eating, and it's especially great if they have muscle or joint problems, and you want your dog to have a happy and healthy life.

Just like people, some dogs don't drink enough water sometimes. If you can get your dog to drink more water, it will be much better and healthier for them. You can get one of the bowls from the pet supply store that gives a continuous supply of cool water, and your dog might enjoy it even more!

11. When Your Border Terrier Has Separation Anxiety, and How to Deal With It

Separation anxiety can happen in any dog, at any age, and for any reason. Doctors are not totally sure why this happens, but they agree that is happens more in dogs that were not properly nurtured as puppies, had new moves, or a new schedule. The dog might be moved around as a puppy, and these things can make a dog have separation anxiety.

Some of the things a dog might do could be excessive, like: howling, barking, whining, pacing, chewing, scratching, digging, urinating and defecating. As the time goes on, the systems become worse, the dog might break his teeth, rip his or her nails, and injure themselves. It seems to happen in pets that did not have much socializing as puppies.

One good way to teach your Border Terrier something good, is to find a quiet place for just you and the dog, and get them to relax by you. When you have them relaxed, give them a treat. You can do this and slowly back away, and put more distance in between you and the dog, slowly separating the two of you.

Another good technique, is be misleading your dog. They might be accustomed to your car keys shaking, meaning you are leaving, or you putting on your jacket, or other signs your dog might read, that lets them know you are leaving.

Try picking up your car keys several times a day, and not leave. Put your jacket on, and take it back off, several times a day. Try to break up your dog's regular routine pattern that you might not even think about. Your dog might already have a routine, that you subconsciously, don't even realize it.

When you come home, pretend that you don't even notice the dog, until he or she has calmed down, and then when they have relaxed, give them a treat or praise.

Another way is to give your dog some excitement. Could you imagine being cooped up all day long, while your owner is out working, and you have to play with the same old toy, day in and day out? If you turn the lights on 30 minutes early, or give your dog a new toy, with a secret treat inside, that will keep them occupied, and spice up their day. If you were a pet, would you not want to be treated that way?

Remember, young dogs still have lots of energy. If you come home and find your favorite chair in threads, you might want to consider increasing your younger dogs exercise pattern. They should be exercised twice a day, from 30 to 45 minutes each time.

You could teach them commands; teach them to play fetch, and other good times. Your Border

Terrier needs plenty of exercise to feel like a dog. Most dogs were breed for a certain job. A herder, a Shepard, a hunting dog, and more. A dog has these instincts in their blood; you need to make sure they get plenty of exercise.

12. When Your Border Terrier is Afraid of Loud Noises

If your Border Terrier has a fear of loud noises, gun shots, fireworks, thunderstorms, and other loud noises, it is a very common among dogs. If he or she is displaying signs like shaking, trembling, hiding, trying to run away, barking, urinating or uncontrollable pooping, these could be some of the signs.

You can sometimes treat this with behavior modifications, general change of environment, and even prescription medicines.

One of the best ways to make the dog better, is to change his or her own living environment around. You should increase the dogs daily exercise program, to make him physically more drained.

Give your pet his or her own space. Pets love to feel secure and protected. Try to make the a crate or sleeping area, that gives them comfort, and has some walls up around them, so they don't feel like that have to worry about things coming at them from all directions.

Dogs usually like to find nice places to relax and sleep. Like under chairs, tables, and places where they feel safe. Where they can sleep, and still keep one eye open, to make sure they stay out of harm's way.

Give your Border Terrier a more noise friendly atmosphere. You could turn on a radio, or run a fan or other mechanical noise maker that is peaceful and continuous. This is good if the dog can hear noise outside, like kids yelling and playing, or other dogs barking, or construction going on. It helps tone down the noise with other continuous noise, to calm the dog.

Don't overly give your dog extra added attention, like petting him or her longer, they might interrupt that as a good reward for acting bad, just treat your dog normally.

One fun way to try and teach your dog not to be afraid, is to give him or her their favorite treat or snack, each time the loud noise is going to come. If it is a thunderstorm, each time the loud bang comes, give your dog a treat, they will look forward to more thunderstorms!

If you want to train your dog not to be afraid, you can obtain CD's or downloads from the internet of thunderstorms, fireworks, gun shots, etc....and begin by letting your dog listen to these sounds at low volume. You will gradually increase the volume over time, and give your dog a treat when she does not freak out to the sound. Slowly increase the volume each training session, then slowly do less and less training, until your Border Terrier does not have any more fear of the loud noises.

If this does not suit you, there are medicines available from your veterinarian, that you can give to your dog before a storm or load noises, to calm him or her down, the old fashioned way, with prescription drugs.

You should be able to find noises on line very easily, with all the major search engines, just type in thunderstorm sounds, and you will be on your way!

13. How to Stop Your Border Terrier from Jumping Up on People

It is your dog's way of getting your attention, and the best way he or she knows, is jumping up on you when they see you, and want to greet you and get some attention from you.

This is almost always cute when your Border Terrier is a puppy, but when he or she gets bigger, that would get old really fast! You need to teach your puppy not to jump up and get excited when they see you.

Some of the best ways to teach your Border Terrier not to jump up on people, and you don't want guests and family members avoiding your dog that jumps up on people, now do you!

The best way to curb this is to not be excited when you see your dog, and don't make eye contact. When your dog goes to jump up on you, turn your body so he or she slides down. Keep doing this, and don't talk to the dog, just use your body language. Keep turning to the side until your dog finally settles down, and then when he or she is standing calm, give them praise for being calm.

Your Border Terrier should learn to be calmer, and they will get the praise they desire, much sooner. Make sure you have all the other family members on board, if one person lets the dog jump up, he or she will be confused, so get the whole family into the training program!

14. How to Build a Whelping Box for an Border Terrier or Any Other Breed of Dog

How to build a whelping box for your Border Terrier, or any other size dog for that matter, just change the sizes. You can determine what size whelping box you need, by making sure your dog has plenty of room to walk around the whelping box. The purpose of the whelping box is to make sure that the mother does not get one of the puppies lodged between her and the box, and squeezes them to death.

Border Terrier's, or any other large size dog, can easily smoother their young if they get laid on. I think the best way to make a nice whelping box for a Border Terrier is to take a full sheet of 1/2 inch plywood, and cut it in half. The floor will be a 4 x 4 piece, and use 2 x 2 woods to make a frame on the inside and along the edges for a nice look.

Take 6 inch wide PVC piping you can buy from any hardware store, and cut 6 inch pieces off of the PVC, and used them for the legs inside. Use plastic PVC elbow joints to connect them together to a perfect 4 foot square that you could raise and lower pretty easy into the whelping box.

When you have the plastic PVC piping inside the box, it makes it harder for the mom to lay down against the sides of the box, when she is feeding her puppies, and if one gets stuck behind her when she moves around all the time, it gives the puppy that added air-vent below that keeps the moms weight off the puppy, and the puppy can survive.

15. How to Teach Your Border Terrier to Sit

Teaching your puppy or dog to sit does not have to be hard at all. The Sit command is a great tool to make your dog behave, and not get hurt if something is going on, and you want them to sit to be safe.

It does not matter if you have a puppy or a dog, you can easily teach him or her to sit on command. You just need to remember, that not every dog will pick things up on the first time, so make sure you have some patience while training.

To teach your puppy or dog to sit, it is important to remember not to do this if you are in a bad mood or frustrated, it is not a good time to teach your dog to sit. Some dogs will learn faster than others, and some will pick it up right away, so just have some patience with them.

You might want to try to teach your dog the sit command, when he or she is getting hungry. That way they will want to get the treats you are giving to them when they do good.

Find a good quiet spot, where there are not distractions from other people and animals. Later you will want to add these distractions in so your dog can learn to sit. Even on a city sidewalk, or at the city park, you want your dog to behave when they are supposed to.

You would want your dog to be standing in front of you, and then with a piece of treat in your fingers, show the dog the treat, and keep it about nose level. If you keep it to high, the dog might try to jump to get the treat.

Wave the treat from the nose towards the tail, and then say the word Sit, while you move the treat back over the dog's head towards their tail. They should sit down while looking at the treat, and when they sit, say Good Dog, and give them the treat.

Your dog should get used to staying in the sit command, until you give the command "Come" or "Free" or another word you might like to use with your puppy or dog.

You would want to teach your dog with treats and praise, and then slowly wean your dog off of the treats, and stick to praise and love. You should not put your dog in the sit hold for very long at the beginning, so your dog does not get bored right off the bat.

Continue practicing with your dog several times a day. Make sure you exchange the treats for praise, and your dog will be much safer when you need them to sit and wait for you, when you give the command.

16. Why Your Border Terrier Needs a Good Soft Bed to Sleep In

You would want to give your new Border Terrier puppy, or any adult Border Terrier dog, a nice big soft bed to sleep in. Border Terrier's are very nice dogs, and if they sleep on the hard ground or floor, they get callouses on their body, just like camels do, and it is not good for them.

Border Terrier's have such wonderful bodies, they need a soft place to lie down, and you should make sure they have a comfortable place to sleep.

Usually a dog that is sleeping on a hard surface, gets calluses on their bodies, and if it gets worse, they call that Hygroma, which can become infected, and filled up, and need medical attention. The best way to avoid this is to give your Border Terrier a nice soft bed. They are going to be a good dog, and fun, and you don't want them to be in pain later in life.

The pet business if filled with tons of different types of soft plush beds for puppies and dogs. Give your Border Terrier the bed he or she deserves, and they will love you for it!

It is not uncommon for adult Border Terrier dogs to sleep twice as long as people threw out the day and night. Your Border Terrier spends a lot of time sleeping, and if he or she has any arthritis or joint problems, they even have special orthopedic beds for older dogs.

Your Border Terrier will appreciate having a nice soft comfortable bed to call his or her own. Just like you enjoy a nice soft mattress to sleep on. Your Border Terrier deserves the same from you, and being that they are such a large size breed dog, they need it even more!

17. How to Stop Your Border Terrier from Running Away or Bolting Out the Door

It is not good at all for your Border Terrier puppy or dog to try to run away every chance they can, or bolt out the door whenever you open it!

This could be one of the worst things for your puppy or dog, as they could get lost or hurt, and you don't want that! The reason they like to run away is many different reasons, and if you can curb some of the reasons, it will make it much better for you and your puppy or dog.

Dogs are usually rewarded when they break out and run away and explore. They can find other dogs they can run with sometimes, or a cat they can chase down the street or up a tree. They might see a child that they never saw before, and wants to be petted by them. They might find a mate dog out there, and they want to go to them.

They could tip over the neighbors trash cans, and find interesting things to rummage thru. There are just all sorts of reasons a dog gets rewarded when they break out, or bolt out the door and take off on you, but still so dangerous!

Whatever the reason your Border Terrier is trying to break out, if you can contain some of the ways and reasons, it will make it much easier for you. For example: if the fence is loose in a certain spot, and he or she gets out there, by all means, fix it!

If the dog can see the mail delivery person coming each day, maybe you could put some tarps up so your dog cannot see out, or even moving the mail box to a different location so you dog does not see it anymore. You need to take away the temptation that gets them wound up in the first place.

You want to make it less inviting for your puppy or dog to break out, than to stay around and stay home. If you take away some of the obstacles, and make it harder for them to break out, that is good. You also want to make their desire to leave and runaway less too.

Some dogs just have a natural instinct to want to get away and be with the pack, be it dogs or humans. It's a natural instinct, and you can curb it, but you can't take it out of your dog.

You can learn a few home trick remedies, but nothing would be as good as you and your dog attending dog obedience classes together! You would learn much more in detail, and your dog would respect you, and wait for your guidance. It would want to please you, rather than bolting out the door on you.

Some little tricks you can do yourself, would be to be by the door, and you open the door when your dog comes, if he or she stops at the door and does not go out, you give them praise and a treat.

If he or she bolts from the door, you get them back, and then you do it again. This time, you let the door almost come closed, but you keep it open just a little bit. When the dog sits or stays and the door is still partly open, you give them a treat and praise again. Repeat this until you have the dog sitting in front of the door, and he or she does not go out, and you give them praise and a treat, until you could rely on praise only.

The only time the dog should want to go thru the open door, is when you go first, and tell the dog to "Come" and he or she will follow you. If you never go out the door or call them, they should stay inside, unless called.

Any dog that breaks out of his or her yard, or bolts from an open door, can end up being a tragic situation for the dog, especially if there are passing cars nearby. You want to take care of this problem immediately, before your puppy or dog gets hurt or killed.

18. Some Helpful Tips for Raising Your Border Terrier Puppy

Before you bring your Border Terrier puppy home, you might want to get things ready for him or her. Some of the things you might want to get would include:

Some dog crates, one or two for the house, and one for the car. You would want to get some fencing for the back yard, and as you know, Border Terrier are going to be really big dogs when they grow up! You might as well get the heaviest duty dog gear you can buy, it will be worth it!

You would want to get your home and yard ready just like you would for a new baby almost. You would want to puppy proof your home, nothing that would hurt the puppy should be out, and all cabinets should be locked.

For outside the house, all pools and hot tubs should be fenced in, and all gates should be locked and double checked. A Border Terrier can really put a lot of weight into something, if you think they might get out, they probably can, so make it even tougher, it's a Border Terrier !

Collars and leashes, you would actually need several, for training purposes. A short one for training and a long one for walks you go on. You should not leave a collar on a puppy while unsupervised, it could get caught and choke the puppy.

A collar should be used only when training, but they are common on most every dog, just make sure you have a good fitting one, and watch your puppy, to make sure he or she does not get it caught, a collar should not be left on, but dog owners do it all the time it seems, so just be extra careful.

You should never have to yell or scream, or get carried away when trying to train your Border Terrier. If you feel he or she is not moving forward, take a break, and try it again in a bit. Make sure you are not the one who is trying too hard. To puppy will learn the commands, over time, no puppy gets it all right the first time, there will be mistakes, but in the long run, you will have a much better trained dog. One you and your family can live with for many years to come!

While your puppy is still young, you should enroll yourself and your new puppy in as many dog obedient classes that you think you could handle. This will be the best experience for both you and your puppy, and you both will bond much better together, and get the most out of it. For the long haul, it is totally worth it!

Hopefully your puppy has already seen the vet before you even brought him home, just for a checkup at least. You should at this time, find a reputable vet in your area, and set your new puppy up for regular visits and exams all puppies and dogs need to have on a regular basis.

The first day you bring you new puppy home, try to make it when you have plenty of time off of work or school, so that the puppy is not immediate left alone, and insecure. It is best to spend plenty of time with the new puppy, especially the first couple of days.

If you can take a sock or towel with you, and let the mother and any other siblings roll around on it, it would be a good comfort blanket to help your new puppy adjust in his new home.

Your puppy might whine, whimper and cry the first couple of nights, this is natural really. It will go away eventually, as this is how the baby is raised by its mother. It whines when it cries for its mother, when it wants to eat, and is crying out for attention.

That is where the towel or sock with the mothers scent rubbed on it, comes in handy to put inside the crate. You would also want some good solid stainless steel bowls for food and water. You should check with your vet on a proper food and feeding time, usually twice daily, at the same times, but some vets recommend different diets for your Border Terrier , so check with your vet first.

Teach your new Border Terrier puppy to be a part of the family. Border Terrier dogs like to be included with the family, they are not that happy if just left in the back yard, they like to be included with the family, so keep that in mind and have fun with your new Border Terrier puppy!

You can teach your new puppy to go to the bathroom outside. You need to take your new puppy outside several times a day. A puppy cannot tell you when they have to go pee or poop, they just go. It is your responsibility to know to take the puppy outside, since they will have to go to the bathroom several times each day.

When you take your new puppy outside, teach them to eliminate in a certain spot, and then give them a treat and praise. Continue to do this, each time you take them outside, tell them to go "potty" and wait for them to go. As soon as they are done, reward them with praise and a treat, and take them back inside.

When take your puppy outside to go to the bathroom, when you take him or her out, just stand still, and let the dog do their business. When they are finally doing their business, while they are doing it, just stand there, and say, "Good Potty" "Good Baby" and talk sweet to them, until they are done.

When they are done, give them praise and a treat. Continue doing this until you only use praise, and the dog will learn to go outside, and do his or her businesses quickly, and then back inside.

Under no circumstances should you ever leave your new puppy unsupervised. If you have to do something, he or she should be in their crate, safe and sound.

19. How to Socialize Your Border Terrier Puppy

All dogs should be socialized as puppies, before they are 16 weeks old. This is the most important time in a dog's life. This is the time that will shape them, and determine what kind of friendly dog they will turn out to be.

This is the time your puppy should get to know people, and other dogs and animals. This is the most important part of a puppy's life, and will determine how his or her behavior is when they grow up, and what type of personality they will have.

This is the most important time to get close and bond to your Border Terrier puppy, and introduce your puppy to things in his or her life. You may introduce your puppy to rides in cars, or meeting new people, or going on a walk in the park.

Your puppy will also be meeting new surroundings and things on his or her own, like plants, wild animals, birds, cats, things they might come across on their own, without you, so they need to be prepared for life.

You want your new puppy to adjust well to his or her new world. You don't want to leave them in a kennel all day, which would not be good for them, or you.

Every single puppy needs to be socialized so they have a good understanding of their environment, and all the things that go on around them. No matter where you obtained your puppy from, all puppies need to be socialized.

The time to socialize your puppy is up to 16 weeks old, after that, it's almost too late. You don't want them to start having problems like separation anxiety, excessive barking, chewing up your favorite items, urinating and defecating in the wrong spots.

If you plan to take your puppy or dog to obedience training classes, you will have a much more enjoyable time if your puppy is already familiar with things. You should take the time to socialize him or her, so they can have an excellent opportunity of being the best dog you want them to be!

You want to socialize your puppy, because when he or she is older, you want them to get along well with humans, other animals, and society in general. You don't want a puppy that hides or is scared of every little thing around him or her.

You don't want a puppy or dog that barks at every moving thing, or anything else like that. Every single person the dog comes in contact with, will be a sign that the puppy that did not get socialized properly at an early age. Give your puppy the love and respect it deserves, and have fun with him or her also while doing this socializing; your dog will love you for it later!

A big reason some of the dogs in the United States have to be euthanized each year is just for the simple fact the dog did not get socialized when he or she was a puppy. And for that sad fact, the puppy or dog just did not have the skills to act appropriately in family, public, or tough situations.

It's a poor fact, that if most all the dogs had been properly socialized as puppies, they would have been much gentler and well behaved dogs when they are grown up. It's not that hard to socialize your new puppy, and it can be fun and rewarding!

You don't really want your do go grow up, where you just leave them in the backyard, and they don't know how to interact with the family, and are a nuisance to the neighborhood in general. One that destroys or digs holes all over your backyard, you have a choice when you get your puppy. You can make him or her responsible, friendly, well behaved, and good natured dog.

It's nice when you have a dog you can trust, and everyone should be able to trust their dog. You want your dog to be able to make rational decisions when he or she is out and about with you. He should be capable of being around lots of people, without jumping up on all of them, and barking nonstop at them.

From the day your new Border Terrier puppy is born, the mother has already started the process for you. When she has the litter, she will make sure she licks each one, to stimulate them, and they can urinate and defecate, and the mother will take care of this, it is natural for them to do that.

As the pups get older, the mother will use smell, sounds, and body language to teach the pups natural skills. This is also the time when the mother might discipline her puppies; don't be alarmed, this is natural also.

The puppies learn from each other while together in the litter. They play, wrestle, and generally learn to live with each other and get along, and get to know each other.

When your puppy is roughly 7 to 8 weeks old, this is the crucial time to play with them, with human hands, with human touch and smells. This is also a good time for the breeder or owner to start puppy on household training.

You do not want your Border Terrier puppy or dog to be afraid of humans when they grow up. It is extremely important to spend some quality time with your puppy, just playing, hugging, and loving him or her. You want them to get used to you, and other members of the household as well.

Most new puppies arrive at their new home around 8 weeks old or older. When your new puppy arrives, you want to immediately start socializing them with everything around them. You want to also remember not to give them something that will scare them too much, or damage them. You would not want to immediately introduce them to an aggressive dog which is too aggressive for them, or one that could scar them for life. Just use common sense when dealing with your new puppy.

If you have a big giant hole in your backyard, you would not want to just let your new puppy go, and find the hole by accident. You would want to introduce your puppy to his new surroundings with a tour, so he or she would feel safe, but still interested and alert.

It is good to introduce your new Border Terrier puppy to a chew toy at this time. This will be used for training purposes. You should pick up your puppy and give him or her, the love all puppies' desire. Rub their belly, scratch their head, talk to them gently, and your new puppy will love it so much, you will too!

Now that your new puppy is home, it is important to start to teach him or her some basic commands right away. They should learn commands like it, stay, down, etc....

This is the time you want to introduce your puppy to lots of new experiences, like loud radios, kids playing and yelling, household appliances that make noises, like vacuum cleaners, televisions, dishwashers, lawn mowers, etc...

It's good to let your new puppy discover for him or herself, while you give good supervision. Let them walk around and discover the plants in your yard, the toys in your kid's bedroom, and the tools in the garage. Don't let them get hurt, but let them explore, so they are not afraid of their surroundings.

If your dog is going to be living in a high rise, or on a boat or yacht, get them used to elevators, or getting on and off the boat safely. Take your puppy out for walks and let them meet other dogs on leashes. Let people stop and pet your dog, you don't want your dog to grow up to be afraid of people, and then bite them out of fear!

It is good to introduce your new puppy to as many people as you can, between 8 and 16 weeks old. This is the stage that it is most important to socialize your new Border Terrier puppy with people. Encourage them to be gentle with your puppy, to touch, to play with, to pet, and to give treats, in a non-threatening manner.

It is not recommended to take your new puppy to off leash dog parks, as some parks have many dogs. Some of the dogs will not have been vaccinated, and it is still your choice, but you would probably not send your kids to school, with other kids that have not been vaccinated, if you knew about it.

Don't assume all the dogs at the off leash dog park have been socialized properly, and they are all vaccinated, so just use caution around dog parks.

If you want to teach your puppy or dog to ride in the car with you, take him or her on short trips at first. If you put a new puppy or dog in a car, and take it on a trip across the country, the puppy or dog might never want to get back in the car again!

Take short trips, and make the first couple to fun places! If your dog's only ride is to go to the vet, or somewhere else unpleasant, they will associate that ride with unpleasant things, so make it happy for them!

20. How to Stop Your Border Terrier Dog from Excessive Barking

If your Border Terrier puppy or dog is barking excessively, it could be from many different things. He or she could be getting caught on, or under a fence. He or she could be barking at other dogs in the neighborhood, or they could be lonely and feel depressed.

Dogs bark for many many reasons really. It would be impractically to think that your puppy or dog would never bark again, because some barking is actually good for a dog, and you!

Dogs bark to alert their owners of danger, or a suspicious person lurking around. But a dog that just barks and barks, and you don't seem to know why, not only bothers you, but it usually always disturbs the neighbors as well.

One of the first things you need to find out is why your dog is barking in the first place. Does he or she see a squirrel or cat in a tree every day, and bark at that? Or does your puppy or dog not get enough exercise, and is left alone outside for long periods of time, and they are barking from boredom. After you find out why they are barking, it is much easier to correct the problem then.

Puppies will naturally bark if they are playing and running around, it is in their nature to playful bark, and that is normal. If you cannot notice what your dog is barking at, sometimes they can see or smell things that you cannot, so you might need to take a closer look again. Maybe there is a small rodent or pest, that is so fast, that you don't see them, but your dog does.

You should also make sure you have your Border Terrier puppy or dog checked out by a vet, to make sure he or she is fine, before you try to correct the problem.

It is good to have a nice place for your dog to sleep, like a dog house, a dog bed, and a nice place to make their own. You would not like it if you had to sleep outside, and no one gave you a house or bed to sleep in, so be good to your dog.

Here are some ways to help curb your dogs barking. If your dog is barking, and you open the door to let him or her in, you are just reinforcing them to bark, each time they want to come inside. When they bark, they know you will come to the door and let them in, and the barking is working for them.

If you go to the door and stand there and scream at them like a raving lunatic, they will think you are joining them in the celebration, and they will want to bark even more! You are barking to them, so they want to bark also, and join in!

If your Border Terrier puppy or dog is barking and you come and baby him, and give him or her treats that is no good. They will take that as a sign that barking is what they need to do, to get more attention from you, so you should never reward this type of barking.

There are several ways to teach your dog that barking is not rewarded. If you are gone all day, and you are aware that your dog barks excessively while you are gone, he or she most likely thinks that if they keep barking, you will show up. Eventually when you show up, you immediately go to the dog, and the barking might stop then. In your dog's mind, he or she has been barking to bring you home, and it worked, you are home finally.

To cure this type of barking, when you get home, do not immediately go to your dog. Let the dog know that you are not rewarding him for barking. Do not go to the dog until after he or she has settled down, and then you can go to him or her, after the barking has stopped and does not start again for a bit.

If your dog barks when the phone rings, or your cell phone goes off, teach them to ignore it. You could do this by having a friend or family member call your phone repeatedly, and you just sit there and don't answer it. With repetition, your dog will bark less and less, and then get bored with the phone all together.

One of the easiest things to remember when training your dog is to praise or reward your dog when he or she does something you like, and give a negative response to something you do not like. Over time, your dog thru repetition will learn what is acceptable, and what is not acceptable. He or she will be a much better member of the family, and it will be good for them also!

There are several ways you could train your dog not to bark when you leave your home. You would need something loud, like a can of rocks, or marbles inside the can, or a garden hose, and you would use these for the negative suggestions. You would leave your home, and then you quietly come back, and just hide outside somewhere in front.

When you hear your dog barking, use the hose to just put the nozzle over the fence, and squirt him or her, or throw the can of rocks or marbles in their general direction, careful not to actually hit them. The loud noise will scare them, and they will associate the barking with getting wet, or having loud noises come at them, they will eventually tire of the barking.

You could also use a treat and the command "Quiet" or "Stop". When your dog is barking, you give the command "Quiet" and when he or she stops barking, you give them a treat and praise, and eventually you would just give them praise.

With just about any dog, it will never happen overnight. It takes consistence and patience. Your dog will make great progress, and then fall back sometimes, that is only natural. They will move forward again, with patience and good dog training, you can make your dog an excellent family member.

Sometimes a dog likes to bark at a mail delivery person, or delivery person that comes around. In your dog's eyes, this person is coming into their territory and is an intruder, an unwelcome guest, and your dog barks continuously at this person. The person usually does leave in a short period of time, and the dog thinks that his barking has made the intruder go away, and he or she has done a good job!

If you wanted to cure this type of barking, and you were friends with your mail person or delivery person, you could tell them your training method, and give them a bag of snacks to carry with them. Each time they would come to your house, they could give the dog a snack over the fence, and the dog would come to think of this person as a welcome guest, instead of an intruder, and the barking would settle down after a bit.

The best way to train any dog is for you and your puppy or dog to enroll in obedience classes together. You will have a much better understanding of just basic dog techniques, and you would bond with your dog even more!

21. When Your Border Terrier Has Dog Food or Toy Aggression Tendencies

If you give your new Border Terrier puppy or dog, a bowl of dog food, and then they growl at you, or try to get between you and the food bowl, they have a dog food aggression. When they have a food aggression, sometimes that carries into toys and playthings also they like to be over protective of.

When your dog shows this type of aggression, he or she is telling you that they are the alpha male dog, and you are not. You have to change this behavior right away, before it gets out of control.

Your dog might not even be aware that he or she is doing this. They might see you as the bad person, because you come and always take things away from them. They might consider their food or toy something you want to take from them, and they want to protect it from you.

Your Border Terrier might think that he might not get any more dog food when what you gave him or her is gone, so they growl at you when you get close, because they don't want you to get it. Each time your dog growls and you back away, it reinforces their bad behavior. They think they are being rewarded by you backing off and leaving them alone, they won the battle in their mind.

If your Border Terrier is sharing a food bowl with another dog and being aggressive, it is best to simply use two food bowls, and separate the dogs while they eat. If your dog seems like he might bite, it is best to stay back, and then correct the problem by making them work for the food.

One way you could teach your Border Terrier puppy or dog is, you could put the food bowl down on the ground empty. The dog will look at the empty food bowl, and be a little bit confused, and then look up at you. You would be in charge now, you could add some food to the bowl a little at a time, and get down close to your dog, and bond with him or her while they are eating.

You should get your puppy or dog used to you touching and petting him or her while they are eating. They should get used to human touch, but be very careful, use caution; you want to get your Border Terrier used to you at meal time.

If your dog is showing you signs of aggression, you could slowly and carefully hand feed your dog. You could use this time to teach him or her "Stay" and "Sit" commands.

You could walk by your dog's food bowl, and while he or she is looking, throw in a treat every now and then, your dog will look forward to you coming around their food bowl and leaving treats or snacks sometimes, and you will be an invited guest.

You could also substitute their food, you simply take the food bowl of food away from them, and then put down something better they would love to eat, and then they get the idea of giving something up, to get something even better from you!

You need to be gentle with your puppy or dog; Yelling or screaming your lungs out is not going to help the situation. Be persistent, and over time, you can teach your puppy or dog to not be so aggressive at meal time, or with their favorite toys. It is always a good idea to enroll yourself and your puppy or dog into obedience classes.

22. What You Should Know About Fleas and Ticks

Fleas, Ticks, Mites and Lice are some outer parasites that will drive your dog and you both crazy. It will involve your puppy or dog constantly scratching and biting trying to get the fleas and other parasites off of them. When you see your puppy or dog using their hind legs to scratch their ears, and using their teeth to try and dig into their skin, it's a pretty good sign they have fleas or a more serious problem.

You can usually get rid of most parasites like fleas and ticks with good quality shampoos and more. One of the things you need to remember is that the eggs that these little parasites leave behind, can take from days to weeks to months to hatch. You need to make sure you kill all the eggs on bedding materials and other places your pet frequents and stays.

Fleas are a common problem for puppies and dogs, and they are known to carry and transfer tapeworms sometimes. A good flea spray or shampoo, or other products should work fine. They do have other brands that you usually apply once a month, that usually will take care of the problem the best, and are on the more expensive side, but well worth it.

You should not use any chemicals on pregnant or nursing mothers, as this could harm the puppies or new born litter.

Ticks are a problem as they can carry Lyme disease and other diseases. Dogs usually get these from trees and bushes, as the parasites fall onto the dog's hair, they then attach themselves to the skin, and suck the blood, and sometimes will suck the blood of humans as well.

If you see a tick on your dog and you want to remove it, do not just pull on it. The head might snap off and stay imbedded into your dog's skin. Use pet shop oil for removing ticks, and try and drown and suffocate the tick, and then use tweezers to wiggle the tick back and forth until the whole body becomes free.

If your dog gets lice, you will be able to spot them pretty easily. You would usually need to get a good quality shampoo or insecticide for lice from your local pet store, and it will usually take several applications to make sure they are gone.

If your dog has mites, it is best to take them to the veterinarian for a checkup, and get special medications for your type of mites. There are many different kinds of mites, so your vet should be able to identify them. Left untreated, it will get worse and worse. Some of the mites to look for are around the ears, with dark spots that looks like small scabs, but are actually mites eating your dog........Some mites you cannot see unless the vet uses a microscope, and for this reason, you should take your dog in right away if you suspect mites, and to help get rid of your dog's discomfort.

23. How to Stop Your Border Terrier Puppy or Dog from Biting

It is natural when puppies are young, to want to bite on something, especially if they are still teething. A young puppy whose teeth are breaking thru their gum lines, will want something to chew on. They will chew on a person's hand to help the teething pain go away, just like babies like to chew on teething rings.

When puppies are playing, they are going to want to snap and bite, but that is because they are playing, and it is completely natural when they do this. The sooner you can teach your puppy or dog not to bite, the better!

It is not a very good practice to play tug-a-war or chase your puppy around the house or yard type games. This will only make the matter worse in most cases. The puppy or dog will get all excited or scared, and his natural instincts will take over, and that might include biting or snapping at you.

You should never smack or hit your puppy, especially in the face. They might end of being afraid of you, or worse, they might think of you as a threat, and then try to bite you!

The other reason a puppy or dog might try to bite you, is they are trying to prove their dominance over you. Just like they are the alpha male dog, and you have to take care of this problem right away, before someone gets bit. If you do not teach your puppy to not bite, he or she will not know, and think it is acceptable behavior. You as the puppy or dog owner, have to put a stop to it right away.

If your puppy starts to bite your hand or foot, give them the command "No" and then replace your foot or hand with a chew toy. You need to teach them that biting you is unacceptable behavior.

24. What to Expect Before and During Your Dog Having Puppies

Dogs will usually give birth roughly 63 days after breeding. This is the time you would want to get things ready for the new mother. You would want to build a whelping box, so the mother has a nice safe place to raise the puppies.

Before the mother gives birth, she will usually start digging, scratching, trying to find a place to hide, to make a place like a den to give birth, as their natural instinct will take over. I have seen a dog in the woods give birth with no help from a human. When I got there, she had cleared a spot in the leaves, and pushed it all away, and made a small den, and her 5 puppies were doing fine, and all were healthy.

You would not want your dog to have puppies in the woods, but that was a site I witnessed. You would hopefully have a whelping box make up for your dog, that has safely rails inside, so the mother does not squeeze any of the puppies, and she can't lean up against them, and smoother then by accident.

It is better if you are with the mother, while she is giving birth. You mostly need to be there, in case the cord is wrapped around the puppies head, or the mother cannot get it out herself after trying.

Always let the mother do it herself, if there is a problem, have clean towels and a sterile pair of scissors handy to cut the umbilical cord in case of emergency.

Usually the mother will have one puppy at a time, sometimes pretty quick, and sometimes about an hour apart. When each puppy comes out, the mother will take the sac, and lick it and get it open, and then start licking the baby, and this will get the puppy to breath. Next, the mother will chew part of the umbilical cord off, with a long piece still hanging on the babies, and then she will chew off even more later.

Your dog will appreciate you more, by being with her, and be gentle with her, and telling her she is doing well. If for any reason something goes wrong, you would need to make sure you get the sac off of the puppy, and then take the towel to dry them up quickly, and then rub their chest to try to get some air into them, so they can breathe. You would then take the sterile scissor, and cut the umbilical cord, and then give the puppy to the mother so she can lick her, then put her on one of the teats so the baby can immediately eat.

Depending on how your dog is, and how she feels most comfortable, some dogs will squat and give birth, others will lay on their side, and let them come out that way. Giving birth is a natural thing, you should just be present for emergencies, and to sooth your dog.

A dog out in the wild that has her puppies on her own, will be much more protective of her pups, and maybe even growl or bite you if you try to get close to the puppies. If you are right there in the box with her when she is giving birth and you are helping her, and putting each puppy on a teat, and making sure they all get milk, she will much more likely welcome you into her pack. It will be much easier for you, when it comes time to socialize the puppies.

At roughly 2 weeks, the puppies eyes and ears will be opening, and then not much longer after that, the puppies will be playing with each other, and jumping around, and nursing from mom nonstop almost it seems. You should have your dog checked out by a vet, before giving birth, and after giving birth, and you can also take the puppies in for a checkup.

Mothers will usually start to wean their puppies about 5 weeks of age. You will start your puppies on a feeding schedule, and its' best to search for the proper amount and schedule online, but a little common sense can go a long way.

All puppies need to be vaccinated against puppy diseases at the proper time. You can have your vet do this, and some pet stores offer this service, and sometimes you can administer the shots yourself, but learn before you do that.

All dogs must have a rabies shot, and only a qualified vet can administer rabies shots, and not until the puppy has reached 4 months old, and not any sooner than that. The rabies shot is very important, as is the shots that are typically called either 5 in 1, or 7 in 1.

You would give them in a series, after waiting a certain amount of time. You would give another shot, usually 3 sets of shots, but with anything, you should consult your veterinarian, and make sure you read any directions very carefully, before trying to do it yourself.

I personally have been buying my own shots for years. I usually get them in a box of 25 that I keep chilled, and I buy them on the internet, and they come in a box with dry ice usually, from a well-respected company, one of the biggest I believe. I do see how it has become harder to buy online, and some companies have discontinued selling to the public, so please do some research.

While your dog is pregnant, she will require more food and water, she is eating for several now! When the puppies are born, and right after, your mother is going to be hungry. I suggest you give her some canned dog food, that is easy for her to digest, and lay off the dry bits for a bit, make sure she has plenty of water, and the softer food will be more gentle on her system, she since just gave birth. I find the mothers are extremely hungry after giving birth, just something I notice with raising dogs for over 25 years now.

For the first several weeks, the mother will use her tongue, to stimulate the puppies, and give them bowl movements. The mother will clean and lick up all the accidents the little puppies make, until they get too much for the mother. Usually right around the time she starts weaning them, and you will start feeding them.

Besides keeping everything clean, your job is not that hard for the first 5 weeks, the mother will be the one doing all the work, as you start to feed the puppies, and clean up the box, you will get much more involved, trust me. I've been cleaning up after dogs and puppies for many years that are one reason you teach your dog to go in a certain spot, right from the beginning.

Your dog should already have a regular vet, and he or she should be aware that your dog will be giving birth. If you suspect any unusual activity, or smelly, foul, orange or reddish discharge, or any other thing you might think is wrong, get her to the vet as soon as you can. Don't let your dog go thru any pain, and don't let any of the puppies get hurt if you can help it.

If you use common sense, and read several different articles about dogs giving birth, that is the best way to teach you about it. Don't read one article, read several different opinions; you will learn much more that way.

25. What the Benefits of Micro Chipping Your Dog Are to You

If you've been wondering if micro chipping your dog is a good thing, it is, if you ask me. It's just like anything, if you ask 7 different veterinarian's the same question, you might get some totally different answers and opinions, so just use your common sense.

A microchip that is placed inside your dog, usually between the shoulder blades, and with a syringe that looks pretty much like the one dogs get their shots with. The microchip is about the size of a grain of rice. It is inserted by your veterinarian, and different vets sell different packages, but relatively all the same.

It is really no more painful to your dog then them getting vaccinated. If you ever lose your dog, this is one of the best ways of hoping to get him or her back.

The microchip is basically a transmitter, that the skin just grows right back over, and it stays with your dog, for their entire life. The transmitter does not require any batteries or maintenance. It is embedded with a number the company supplies and your veterinarian will have much more details on, you will have to pay a onetime fee for this service.

When a scanner that a vet or animal shelter should have on hand these days, maybe some smaller out in the country vets still don't have access to one, but if they do, the scanner would make the transmitter give off a signal, that the scanner could read. Since it is universal, injecting the microchip behind the shoulder blades, but over time and years, some dogs may have growth movement.

Millions of dogs get lost every year. One of the best ways to make sure your puppy or dog does not get lost in the first place, is to be a responsible pet owner. Make sure your home and yard is puppy and dog proof, just like you might do for a real baby in your home.

Make sure fences and gates are secure, make sure there are no holes being dug you don't know about. Make sure your dog gets plenty of exercise and care and love, so they don't feel the need to go elsewhere.

If for some reason your dog becomes lost, the collar and tags might get lost or removed, and then it is nearly impossible to find the rightful owner sometimes, and the worst you can imagine might happen. With the microchip, it is not a for sure bet, but your odds are much higher of getting your lost dog back, then if you did not have it.

Hopefully your puppy or dog has a very nice place to live, either indoors or outdoors, and they like their surroundings, and never dream of running or getting away. But if for some reason, they are in heat, or they hear kids playing, or the mail delivery person coming, and they want to escape, or they just get loose by accident. Like a small child leaving the door open, and then they are long gone, that microchip is going to play a much bigger role in finding him or her, and I really hope it works for everyone!

26. How to Get Something Out of a Puppy or Dog's Belly without Surgery

If your puppy or dog has chewed up something and you don't know what to do, you could try this method maybe. But you should always go to, or call your veterinarian first, and let them know what you are going to do.

Now I would not recommend this procedure to anyone really, I just wanted you to know that there is another option out there, before resorting to costly surgery, that could hurt or kill the puppy or dog. For those that do not have the money for surgery, I would not want you to leave something dangerous in your puppy or dog, and this might help you out.

If your dog eats some Christmas tree ornaments, the glass kind, or some metal objects, like small staples, pins, or glass fragments, or anything else that is totally dangerous, there is one other way to get the items out, without surgery.

You would use cotton balls to do this with. You would want to buy some cotton balls, and make sure it is cotton balls, not something on the bag that says cosmetics, as that will have some other type of fibers in it that would not be good for your dog, so make sure you get the ones that say Cotton Balls.

For small size dogs, you would use roughly 2 cotton balls, for medium size dogs, you would use about 3 to 5, and for large size dogs, you can use 6 or more. You would want to cut the cotton balls into smaller sizes. If your puppy or dog swallows glass shreds, from things like Christmas tree ornaments, or other items, you would dip the cotton balls in milk or water, and then the puppy or dog will actually eat it and swallow it. If for some reason your dog does not want to, you can actually force the cotton balls into their throat, and make them swallow it.

As the cotton works its way through the digestion system, it will pick up all the fragments of glass, even the tiniest of ones, and it will get caught in the cotton material. The cotton will protect the inside linings of your dog, so your dog will stay protected. When the puppy or dog defecates, you would want to make sure there is no bleeding, and if there is, take your puppy or dog to the veterinarian immediately.

If you suspect your puppy or dog of swallowing something, you should take them to the vet. If you think you can do it yourself, you could try this method, as the cotton balls are supposed to entangle all the bad stuff, and protect it when it is coming out the dogs body, and then if everything goes well, you have maybe just saved your dog's life. Even if you take your dog to the vet, you could mention this procedure to your vet, as not every vet is up on everything, and no two veterinarians are the same.

27. How to Clean Your Border Terrier s Ears Correctly

Before you start to clean your puppy or dogs ears, you should make sure you do not smell a really foul odor coming from their ears. If it smells pretty bad, they might have an infection and bacteria in the ears, or worse. You should take your pet to the vet right away, because it could be something serious.

It is good to get your dog used to having their ears cleaned on a weekly basis if you can. You never want to use cotton swabs or Q-tips on dog's ears, only cotton pads, the kind ladies use to take their makeup off is best.

You should pick up a good puppy or dog ear cleaning solution from your local pet supply store or veterinarian. Gently pull the ear flap upward to straighten out the ear canal, and then squirt some of the cleaning solution into your puppy or dogs ear. Massage the base of the ear with your thumb and fingers for about 30 seconds, to make sure the cleaning solution gets deeper down into the ear.

Your puppy or dog is going to want to shake their head to get the cleaning solution out of their ears, and just let them do that for a minute.

Next use a damp cotton pad to gently wipe out the dogs ears, and clean them up as good as you can. Make sure you do not put anything down inside of the dogs ears, as this could hurt them, and freak them out also.

To help your puppy or dog relax the first few times, you could gently give your dog a head and ear massage, and gently start exploring and playing with their ears, so that they get used to the feeling of your fingers poking around their ears. Most dogs are heavily sensitive in their ears and feet the most, so be careful not to frighten them, just be gentle and easy.

You should never use peroxide on your dog if it has not been diluted. Pure peroxide can be to harmful to your puppy or dogs ears full strength. Consult your vet when you have signs of foul odors, since dogs ears are one of their keen senses they use.

When you are done cleaning your puppy or dogs ears, make sure you let them air dry, especially if they are long, since it will be harder to dry. Bacteria and other things love warm damp areas to grow, so make sure you get them dry before you let him or her go run off. Keep the ears folded over, to make sure they get good air circulation to dry correctly and not be left damp.

28. How to Stop Your Border Terrier from Eating Their Own Stools

The last thing you want to do is see your Border Terrier eating his or her own feces stools! You would not want any guests or family members over, and your dog does that in front of them!

If your Border Terrier is eating his or her own feces stools, you might want to increase their daily exercise activity and make sure you are feeding him or her, a high quality dog food.

There are chewable treats for dogs, which will make even the worst offender stay away from his or her own feces stools. It goes right thru the intestines of your dog, and out in the stools, with a taste they will hate, but it will not harm them!

The active ingredient is pretty close to red hot chili peppers, and your dog will hate the taste, but the treats do not harm your dog at all. They will not eat their feces stools anymore, thereby taking care of the problem.

This is not to be used in puppies, or dogs that are nursing, or dogs with any medical problems. Ask your vet about dog treats that will stop your Border Terrier from eating his or her own stools, and you could just as easily order it online also if you search for it.

The last thing you want at a party or family get together, is your Border Terrier showing off his bad habits of eating their own feces, it just is not good, and you need to take care of it immediately.

29. How Invisible Fencing Typically Works to Train and Protect Your Dog

Hopefully this will give you a basic understanding on how invisible fencing for your dog should work, and if it is for you, or not for you. Only you can decide if you agree with invisible fencing. Not all yards are the same, and by no means, not all dogs are the same, but it should work for most people that use it correctly.

The system would usually entail you trenching a trench, or digging up the ground along the path you want your invisible fencing to go. Just pretend it is an invisible wall, and where you put the wires, will be where the invisible fencing will be located at.

You would want to check with your local utilities or power company before digging up and installing the wires. But it is not that difficult for the average person, as long as they follow the instructions carefully for the system they purchase.

Your dog would be fitted with a collar that has some sensors that stick out and contact the dog's skin. From what I hear, the dog does not get a shock, but a surprising jolt, and since dogs cannot talk, we will really never know what they feel, until we find a dog that can talk. We can put him or her on television, and they can maybe tell us everything that is wrong with dogs and kids would love that story, but you get the idea!

The way it works is you bury the wires underneath the lawn, so you don't have wire everywhere. You can also run it along wooden fences, but not metal ones, and that could be a boundary wall, so they don't dig out, but you don't have to dig up that section, because a fence is already there, basically making them stop digging out, or jumping up on the fence any more.

The collar would require batteries, and a test period, and training sessions with your dog, so that he or she understands what is desired of them. You have to train them properly about where they can, and where they cannot go in the yard. They do have systems for inside the home for dogs that jump over gates, and you could find that on the internet for inside places.

You would place red flags along the path of the invisible fencing, for training purposes with your dog. Your dog needs to be able to see the invisible lines first. That is what the flags are put in the ground for. A system that is working fine would give the dog several beeps warning him or her that they are getting too close to the fence.

If they do not move back, they will get a shock or surprise jolt, depending on how you look at it, since the dog can't tell us. The part you really need to teach your dog before you let him or her loose or on their own, is to turn away from the fence, and go back.

You could teach them this by turning it into a fun game for both of you. You would train your dog by taking them up to the fence, and when the warning beeping starts to go off, you could turn around and run, and call your dog to come too! Then when he or she comes, you could give them some praise, and teach them to turn back, not go thru it.

Like anything, you would actually need to teach them to go thru it, so they know what they are in for. Walk with them, and when the warning beeping is going off, let them experience the effect of the surprise.

I'm hoping they are getting a surprise rather than a shock, but if this saves them from running out in the street and getting hit and killed by a car or truck. Or getting lose and biting someone, then I believe they need to learn what happens if they don't come back, while you are there, rather than while you are away.

You would leave the red flags up until you think your dog is ready for them to be taken down. As with anything you love, take good care of your dog, and watch them and keep an eye on them. If you just use common sense, and follow the directions on the kit you buy, and don't take any short cuts, do it right the first time, and it will work. Just plan everything ahead of time, and give your dog plenty of time to learn the new system with you, and you both should be happier and safer!

30. Some Items You Should Never Let Your Puppy or Dog Eat

Some items you should never let a puppy or dog eat, because it can harm or kill them, so you should be aware of them. I'm sure most people already know you should never give a puppy or dog chocolate, not even a little piece. Chocolate usually has caffeine in it, and even just a small amount could kill a puppy or dog, or put them into convulsions.

Just like people, some big guys can eat 15 hot dogs, and 5 bottles of beer, and the next guy can't even eat 1 hot dog, and would never finish a bottle of beer, that is just an example really. A puppy or dog is the same way; no two dogs are going to be alike! Some dogs might be fine eating broccoli, and other dogs might bite the bullet from it, so it's just nice to know what kinds of foods could hurt your dog, and this list could change at any time really.

"Some items you would not want to give your dog might include: raisins and grapes, macadamia nuts, walnuts, cooked bones (raw bones are good, cooked bones splinter and can hurt your dog much easier than raw soft fresh bones.) You would not give avocado, onions, garlic, mushrooms, broccoli, tea or coffee, white bread, white potatoes, white rice, peppers, raw spinach and probably some other things your vet might have on a list for your dog."

Granted, some dogs might have been eating some of these products for years, but all young children need to be taught, that giving even the smallest amount of chocolate to a puppy or dog, can be deadly. Even the candy bar wrappers on the ground, a dog might try to lick it up.

Teach children that candy has no place in a dog's life. Some dogs cannot digest broccoli for example very well, and other dogs might be just fine. It is better to find alternative foods, since the world has so many kinds.

The best food of all is food you make yourself, since you can actually see the real ingredients going into it. Some super market dog foods are so full of corn and soy beans, you wonder if your dog gets any nutrition from it, unless he or she eats the whole bag, and that could be the case.

If you learn to fix your dog healthy food at home, and leave out the stuff that might hurt or kill him or her, you would be doing your dog a big favor!

31. How to Make Sure Your Dog is Eating a Healthy Amount of Food

You as the dog owner have the responsibility to make sure your dog is not under fed, or over fed. Some mature dogs can have free food out all day long, and eat just the right amount on their own. Some other dogs just might eat nonstop, and hurt themselves, and then you usually have to stop that, and feed them a measured amount twice a day, so they don't over eat, every dog is different.

Younger puppies and dogs usually are very energetic, and can burn off some steam, but you should still exercise them, and take them to obedience classes if you can. Older dogs get more set in their ways, and tend to sleep more as they get older. Older dogs still need exercise, but not long periods of it. It is best to give them plenty of times to go out and exercise with you, just shorter periods of time.

You can ask your vet what is the best food to give your dog. Each vet will have his or her own opinion, and then try to stick with what they tell you. You can also go online and use a weight chart, and determine roughly how much your dog should be eating daily.

You can measure that amount into their bowl twice daily, and if they are eating it all, you can increase the amount, to control weight gain or loss, just like decreasing the amount you give them. Your vet should be able to tell you what your dog's daily intake should be, and then try to stick to that.

Make sure you have plenty of fresh drinking water available at all times for your puppy or dog. If you leave your dog inside a crate, make sure there is amble water supply. Dogs, just like humans, would prefer a nice cool drink of refreshing water, rather than a drink from old warm water with dog hairs floating in it. Give your dog fresh water as often as you can.

32. Make it Easier and Healthier for Feeding Your Border Terrier

You can make is much easier on your Border Terrier when it comes to eating. Some dogs you can leave their food out for them, and they do not over eat. Other dogs may over eat until they get bloated, or they gobble it down super-fast, and have gas problems and more serious problems.

To find out how much your dog should be eating, you should check with your vet. You could also measure your dog's food, and then feed him or her twice a day. If they eat the whole bowl, give them more next time, if they don't eat it all, give them less each time. You could measure it, and then come up with the right amount for your dog for each meal.

For dogs that gobble down their food so fast, the pet supply places sell dog bowls that have inserts in the bowl, so the dog would have to slow down to eat. You would never want to give your dog just one meal a day. You should feed them twice a day, and at the same time each day, so they can count on their schedule, just like people seem to love, breakfast, lunch and dinner!

For large size dogs, it is harder on them and their joints when they have to bend over to get their head down to the ground to get a drink of water, and that is bad for their joints, especially if they are young still.

Some pet supply stores sell water and food bowls that go in a stand and make it higher off the ground. That makes it easier for your puppy or dog to swallow, as their body is more parallel to the ground while eating.

A raised water and eating bowl, will make your dog more comfortable when eating, and it's especially great if they have muscle or joint problems. You want your dog to have a happy and healthy life.

Just like people, dogs don't drink enough water sometimes. If you can get your dog to drink more water, it will be much better and healthier for them. You can get one of the bowls from the pet supply store that gives a continuous supply of cool water, and your dog might enjoy it even more!

33. How to Clean and Groom Your Border Terrier

It is very important to clean and groom your puppy or dog on a regular basis to keep them clean and sharp looking, and just nice to smell!

When bathing your puppy or dog, make it a fun experience for them each time, and the early your start doing it, the better! This is the time you can inspect your dog completely, so that you can notice any new cuts, scrapes, rashes, or anything that you might not notice when you're just playing with your dog.

This is also the perfect time to inspect your puppy or dogs nails, and to check to see if they are too long and need to be trimmed. Use cotton balls when cleaning the inside of the ears, never use cotton swabs, as you could damage their ears. Check inside of the ears for any foul orders, a sure sign that you need a visit to your local vet. If your puppy or dog shakes his or her head a lot, and try's to scratch at it on a regular basis, your dog could have ear mites, or an infection.

If you do not wash, comb or brush your dog on a regular basis, they could end with mats in their hair, and those are harder to get out. When mats get wet, they are harder to deal with, so you should try to get them out before the bath.

Fleas can be another big problem. Make sure you use good quality flea shampoo, and for serious problems, consult your vet at once. Your veterinarian or pet supply warehouse will also carry some more expensive solutions, that do work very well, that you can usually place on the dog once a month, to cure this problem.

In order to keep water out of your dog's ears while giving him or her a bath, you could put cotton balls just inside the ear canal, so that water does not get inside the ears, and cause a bacterial infection later.

After you get the bath ready for your puppy or dog, you do not want to get water in their eyes or ears. You certainly do not want to put your dog's head underneath the water, unless you want your dog to panic and freak out, not a good idea at all.

Wet your puppy or dogs hair from the head down, and then apply a good quality shampoo, then lather the dog up, rinse and repeat. During the bath, it is good to talk to your dog, and tell them they are doing a good job. They will relax more when they hear the gentleness of your voice.

After you take your dog out of the bath, you do not want to just let him or her go outside, because they will go directly to some dirt, and roll in it, and all your work will be wasted.

You should towel dry them as much as you can, and then let them air dry in a warm place until they care completely dry. Then you should comb or brush them until they are nice looking. If you do decide to use a blow dryer on your dog, make sure you set it on the lowest setting so you don't hurt your dog.

If your dog gets so dirty, or has more mats than you know what to do with, it is best to go to a professional groomer, and let their experience work for you. You might just learn a few tricks for next time by watching them, for when you to do it yourself later.

34. How to Trim a Puppy or Dogs Nails Properly

The first thing you should know about dogs nails is that the blood vessels go down to their nails, and if you cut it to short, it will bleed or hurt the dog.

The part you DO NOT want to cut is called the "quick". That is the part that has the pink color to it in white or clear nails. For dogs with dark nails, it is much harder to see, and you need to be more careful.

It would pay to get a quality pair of nail clippers, if you are not sure, you can ask your vet. You could even have them or your groomer give you a lesson on how to trim the nails yourself. It is not that hard, you just need to be extra careful not to hurt the puppy or dog.

You would be much better off if you teach your dog when they are a puppy, to have their nails clipped. If your dog is walking around and you can hear their nails clicking on the floor, it is time to cut them. Some dog's need their nails cut once or twice a month, other dogs can go longer between pedicures.

Make sure the nail clippers you are using are sharp. You would start at the tip of the nail, and then clip a little bit at a time. When you get close to the quick or pink part, you do not want to cut that.

If you do cut that, and it starts to bleed, use a styptic stick or styptic powder, or even baby powder, and apply pressure until the bleeding stops.

On dark or black nails, it is very difficult to see the pink sometimes, so you want to do just a little at a time. You can use a nail file to file down the rest, and to file off any sharp edges from clipping.

This is also the perfect time to inspect your puppy or dogs feet. Some dogs that play outside, can get the little burs from the plants outside. The little prickly thing gets stuck in their feet, just like a thorn, and can get infected.

I know this from experience, as we had those weeds on our land, and our dog got the smallest one in her foot, and it got infected. The vet gave us antibiotics until the infection was cured, and then I made sure I removed those kinds of weeds from our property.

If your puppy or dog did not have his or her dewclaws removed, then it would need to be clipped also. It could get caught up on something when your dog is jumping around. It is the nail on the inside of the front legs that is a little bit up from the paws, it does not get used, so it might be pretty sharp. Do that one the same way you clip the other nails.

If you don't trim your dog's nails on a regular basis, the quick will start to get longer over time, the part with the blood vessels. Your dog's nails need to be clipped or filed down. If you can hear them click on the floor when they walk, they need taken care of. The dog should be walking on his or her paws, and the nails should not be touching the floor.

If your dog's nails are too long, it can make it hard for them to walk around properly. It is good to have your dog lay all the way down on the floor while you trim the nails. When you are done trimming your dog's nails, you should give praise and a treat to your dog, because you are going to have to do it again sometime, and you want your dog to cooperate each time.

35. The 5 Different Kinds of Worms That Can Harm Your Dog

There are 5 different kinds of worms that can hurt your puppy or dog, and here is a list of them, and what they can do to your dog. There are many different types of medicines and antibiotics for your dog, and not all of them work on each symptom, so it is best to consult your vet for the proper treatment.

One of the easiest ways for puppies and dogs to pick up worms is by them playing or eating their feces matter. It is important to pick up your dog's poop in the backyard all the time on a regular basis, so it can be clean and safe.

Hookworms: Hookworms are not visible from the naked eye. Hookworms hide in the intestines and can be transferred to humans. Hookworms are small thin worms that hook onto the intestinal wall and they suck the blood from the puppy or dog, which can cause anemia, and even death.

These worms actually have teeth that cause bleeding in the intestines. Hookworms will grow to full maturity in the intestines. Hookworms can be spread from the mother's milk right to the pups, so the whole family needs to be dewormed.

The worms like to live in feces matter, and contaminated soil, like the dirt you might have in your back yard you dog likes to play in maybe. If your dog has hookworms, some signs might include: anemia, weight loss, diarrhea, bloody stools and very low energy.

Hookworms could be present, and you won't be able to see them, so you would need to take your pet or a stool sample from your pet, to the vet for a diagnosis.

Roundworms: Roundworms are the most common type of worms in puppies. Just like hookworms, roundworms attack the intestines, and can cause a potbellied look on your puppy or dog.

Puppies can get roundworms from their mother's milk or even from the uterus before birth. They can also pick up the eggs from contaminated soil outside, since roundworm eggs can live up to several years outside in the dirt and soil.

Roundworms can be transmitted to humans, just like hookworms, so it is vital to eradicate them as soon as practical. Roundworms will live in the intestines and will grow to adulthood, and lay eggs that will produce more roundworms.

Roundworms can be seen by the eye in your dog's vomit or stools, and is up to 7 inches long, and will resemble spaghetti somewhat. When your puppy or dog starts to get to many of these roundworms, you will see the potbellied appearance on them, and you may notice vomiting, diarrhea, and weight loss.

Whipworms: Whipworms are one of the harder worms to kill. Whipworms are long skinny shaped worms that live in the dog's colon, and you cannot see them with your eyes.

Whipworms will also attach to the intestines, and cause intestinal bleeding inside your dog. Signs of whipworms could be weight loss, anemia, diarrhea with some blood or a gooey mucus type substance in it, and just a lack of energy.

Tapeworms: Tapeworms get their name, because they look like flat Scotch tape. Tapeworms attack the intestines, and can be seen by the naked eye. The tapeworms will look like a rice appearance in your dog's stools.

Tapeworms can be broken into pieces, and sometimes you can see the worms on your dog's anus and stools, still moving around, with your naked eyes.

Tapeworms are not transmitted directly to humans from dogs, but a human could still be infected. Some signs your dog might have tapeworms would be weight loss, uncontrollable itching around the anus area, lots of pain if you touch their abdominal area, and vomiting.

Heartworms: Heartworms are spread by mosquitoes, when mosquitoes are active, and go from one dog to the next. Heartworms can kill your dog if left untreated, and it is easily preventable. There are no symptoms for heartworms, until it is almost fully advanced.

The heartworms destroy the muscle and tissue of the heart, and can cause heart failure, and kill your dog. One of the best measures these days is to consult your vet for heartworm guard, and you can easily find medications online for your dog's heart, since starting them on a medication is the best practice.

36. How to Deworm Your Border Terrier for Good Health

With the different types of dog worms found, it is important to make sure you put your puppy or dog on a deworming program at the start of 2 weeks old. Some worms you cannot see with the naked eye, and it is important for the puppy and dogs health to be protected against these parasites that infect their bodies sometimes.

Here are some other things you can do to help prevent worms: Try not to let your puppy or dog play with dead animals or rodents, this is where most tapeworms come from. Puppies are prone to tasting their feces matter, so make sure you discourage that, and clean up waste right away. This is the most common way for puppies and dogs to get worms.

Having your dog on a flea prevention program is great, since fleas help spread tapeworms in dogs. The dog park is sometimes not the best place for your dog to hang out. Sure he or she would love it, but some other dog owners do not have their dogs under control. This is an easy place for other dogs to catch stuff, from digging in the dirt, to jumping and licking other dogs.

Usually you will have to take a stool sample to your vet, and they will examine it under a microscope, to see what type of worms your dog has. For heartworms, a blood test is usually required to detect heartworms.

Some dogs may have a small amount of worms that pose no threat to the dog, since some dogs have different immune levels, and for some dogs, just the slightest infestation, could kill them. Too many worms for any dog would be bad, and totally affect their health and wellbeing.

Your dog would have diarrhea, and their shiny coat of hair would become dull looking. Most of the nutrients your dog needs from food would be going to the worms, and your dog would lose energy, and lose weight. The red blood cells would become destroyed and the dog would become anemic.

You can find many different types of dewormers for your puppy and dog from pet stores, to online pet stores, and some of the major retailers of pet products. Dewormers can come in the form of pills, liquid or injection. Make sure you understand how to do it, each company and type of dewormer could have different directions.

Most vets recommend deworming your puppy at 2, 4, 6, 8 and 12 weeks old. Then follow the directions, as some medicines will be monthly, or quarterly, and even semiannually, so ask your vet which dewormer is best for you, or follow the directions closely on the dewormer product your purchase.

37. What You Should Know About Dog Rabies

Rabies is the one of the most preventable diseases almost, just by simply going to your vet, and having your dog vaccinated. In all 50 states it is the law, that all dogs should have rabies vaccinations no sooner than 4 months, and only by a veterinarian.

Some states and towns have different rules about when dogs have to be re-vaccinated from 1 to 3 years annually, with so many districts being different from each other, so you need to check with your town or city.

Most dogs get infected from wild animals that might have the disease, like skunks, raccoons, foxes, coyotes and bats. Most all rabies is transmitted when an infected animal bites another animal that has not been vaccinated. The virus in the saliva inters thru the bite entrance, and travels to the brain where is destroys the dog. There is no known cure for the disease yet, and it is almost always fatal, and the dog will most certainly die from the disease.

There are vaccinations available for humans so they do not get the rabies virus, but that is usually reserved for veterinarians, and people that deal in wildlife, or travel to high risk areas mostly.

If you take your dog to the vet after they are 4 months old, the veterinarian can usually give a low cost rabies shot, and make your puppy or dog safe, and protect others from the disease from spreading.

Lots of pet owners don't get around to getting their pets vaccinated, and that is just one more reason you should get yours done. It is a disease that will destroy your dog, and tear you apart. It is very easily preventable with a simple vaccination, and all states require it by law now.

There are 3 stages of the rabies disease that can affect your dog. Some signs your dog might be infected would and could include things like bite marks, or your dog licking a fresh wound constantly.

The disease would make some dogs that are generally good matured, would have a split personality, and turn violent and vicious. Dogs that are usually aggressive or mean, are now being timid and friendly and calm.

The disease spreads thru the nervous system until it attacks the brain and starts to multiply. There is no cure, and it is too late for your dog after they get the virus. Most vets would recommend uthanization prior to death, to save the dog from the pain and suffering. That alone is worth taking your dog to your friendly pet shop and setting up an appointment, or just walking in when they have a rabies clinic.

Some of the more unpleasant results at the end stage would include the dog's lack of muscle control in the neck and head. This would cause them to drool saliva, since they cannot swallow anymore, and it's almost the end for them. The only way to know for sure if your dog has rabies is after death. They can take a brain sample and put it under a microscope only after the dog has died, to see if it was rabies. They do have other tests, but it is rare to be used.

One of the best ways to keep your puppy or dog protected is use common sense. Take your pet to the vet for their vaccination. When you take your pet out on a hike, or along the river bank, or thru the hills and over the mountains, try to make sure you can keep an eye on them from wild animals. A dog is going to be a dog and investigate things, especially wild animals they find, and that is where the vaccination should have come into play already to protect your dog in the first place really.

38. Some Helpful Healthy and Tasty Homemade Dog Food Recipes

How to make your dog a Healthy Breakfast: Ok, so you have a dog and he is not just another little one running around, pawing you and asking you for a little more love and attention, he demands it!

As cute as it may seem, but as a dog owner, you play the role of just being more than that, you are indeed his parent, his sibling, his cousin, whatever relationship status you name it!

Today we would like to share with you a healthy breakfast option for your dog. Remember, your dog is a growing boy and you may not notice too much, but yes he is indeed growing and would need the best nutrition and care, sometimes more than your own kids.

We would love to give you this recipe and you would for sure love to serve this for your dog, so folks, gather your pen and papers and jot every word down, your dog needs a treat and you got to make one for him this morning.

Ingredients:

1. A bowl of boiled chicken breasts

2. 5 potatoes boiled

3. 250 grams carrots boiled

4. 1 teaspoon turmeric powder (kills the worms and heals internal infections if any)

5. Bay leaves, two only

6. Half a liter of water

7. Half a bowl of cooked rice

Instructions: On a slow fire add the chicken to the water and mix the turmeric and bay leaves. Allow it to boil for twenty minutes, till you see the oily surface of the broth. Now put in the carrots and raise the heat of the cooking dish. Keep stirring and watch how the chicken and carrots blend into one another.

Remove the dish off the fire and allow it to cool. This is when you take the boiled potatoes and mash them into tiny balls and allow them to submerge with the broth made. Your dog would surely love the new recipe and would beg you for more. Once it is lukewarm, pour the contents into the rice and add a little bit of honey if you please. Each of this cookery would last your dog for three meals or more.

Tips and warnings

1. I recommend chicken for dogs without bones; bones break into tiny splinters which rip the walls of the stomach. This can cause internal bleeding and sores, leading to death in some cases.

2. Turmeric should be used not more than a teaspoon in all cooking meals for humans and pets. It kills the worms and prevents further decay of internal injuries if any.

3. Honey is a natural appetizer, makes your dog eat well and helps him digest as well.

Conclusion: Folks, if you would like to try ground beef, or lamb, you can do so. But always remember for such meats, you should boil them twice, since most of it has a lot of worms hidden and can be harmful for the dog. Your dog is going to live healthier and love you more!

When your Dog Loves It Raw: Some dogs like Buddy wouldn't want to eat cooked food, blame it on their natural instincts to love everything raw! No matter how hard you try to make him eat, he just won't touch it. Understanding this predicament of pet owners around the globe, we have a healthy raw recipe which your dog would be thankful for, so we urge and encourage you to use this recipe!

Please be advised this is a tried and tested recipe, however, you should speak to your vet before you think of feeding your dog this new recipe I have for you. So please read on folks, your little baby wants the best nutrition available.

Ingredients

1. Pound of raw chicken or beef (ground to coarse

2. A bowl of veggies, carrots, cabbage, tomatoes and beetroot.

3. Half cup of raw liver or even gizzards would do, whatever is easily available.

4. Cider vinegar not more than half a cup, apple flavored.

5. Garlic pods not more than three.

6. A teaspoon of kelp ground fine

7. Half a cup of white curd

8. Three eggs boiled

9. A bowl of parsley, if you please

10. A teaspoon of honey and turmeric to add flavor and color

Instructions: Please take the veggies and chop them fine, know that dogs don't chew all that much, they swallow. You should also know how your dog eats his meals, if he chews or swallows that is. Store the chopped veggies in the fridge for half an hour. This would help make it crisp and dogs love crispy stuff, it strengthens their teeth.

Next with the meat and liver, over here you can have a mix of raw bones and meat, however, I still insist on no bones, since bones can cause splinters when they break in the dog's digestive tracts and can cause internal injuries over time. The mix of meat and veggies to serve is your take, you decide.

On some days you can put 60:40 and other days 40:60 or a 50:50 as well, the choice is yours.

Add the embellishments on the mix, with chopped boiled eggs, apple cider, parsley etc. Toss it well and make it look yummy, serve at normal room temperatures. This meal could be for three whole meals in a day, so serve as you deem fit.

Tips and warnings: Raw meat enhances muscle strength and development for your dog. This also enables his gums and mouth to be stronger, since he would chew better. Since he would chew more, he would help the digestion process go well down within him. Our boys are the best natural raw meat lovers we could find around, so no worries there, but ensure you wash the meat well, especially if it comes as a stored or packed product. You should ensure the salts and preservatives are washed away, so wash the meat and bones twice.

When Your Dog Has Fussy Food Habits: Sometimes we wonder if teenagers are more stubborn at their eating habits or our pets? Never mind, that would always be a mystery unsolved. Today I would like to tell you about a very nice recipe which I think your King or Queen in your house would love to have.

You don't need to run from pillar to post to find the ingredients, it's all there in your kitchen, so please read on and be well informed on your dog's diet.

Ingredients:

1. A bowl of chicken liver

2. A bowl of carrots chopped and smashed, boiled would be great

3. A bowl of potatoes boiled

4. Cucumbers not more than two

5. A teaspoon of turmeric

6. 2 bay leaves

7. 5 slices of bread

Instructions: On slow fire, you should take a liter of water and put the chicken liver pieces in it. The boiling should be done in fifteen to twenty minutes and you should, while the boiling happens, add turmeric and bay leaves.

Once the broth is made, take the liver out and keep separate. In the broth add the cucumbers and potatoes. Mix this well, adds to it the carrots, and keep stirring for ten minutes aggressively. I say aggressively, so that the flavors combine and the ingredients blend into one another.

Now take the chicken liver and run it in the mixer with a little more turmeric and make it into a paste. Add bread slices crushed into the mixer while the paste is being made. If you want you can add some mint and coriander, not too much, because your dog wouldn't want to have it then.

Finally, add the paste into the broth and bring it back to the slow fire. This would be to bring down the levels of extra water and allow it to turn into a thick creamy pudding.

Serve it when it is lukewarm, so that his tongue doesn't burn and yet the taste remains. Ensure you add a teaspoon of honey into her food at all meals. Honey is an appetizer and would help her eat well and absorb the nutrition at large.

Tips and warnings: If your dog isn't eating too well, check with the vet, she could be having digestion issues. Don't ignore just because he isn't eating, there could be a reason.

If you feel your dog could be allergic to chicken liver, you could try this with ground beef or plain chicken breasts. I recommend no bones at all for the dog, unless specified by the dog's health care expert. If you don't want to bring the water levels down in the broth, allow the extra water to be put into another container and serve that separately as an in between snacking option, dogs love it!

Printed in Germany
by Amazon Distribution
GmbH, Leipzig